THE FUN
TO OX

for Rosina

© Chris Gill 2015

CONTENTS

ASHMOLEAN MUSEUM

The Ashmolean Museum was built in the Classical Style by Charles Cockerell in 1845, at a time when the Victorian Gothic style was becoming fashionable (see the Randolph Hotel opposite the museum and the Martyrs' Memorial nearby). At first, the building housed the University's art collection, but in 1908 it added the objects from the old Ashmolean Museum in Broad Street (now the Museum of the History of Science). The museum has collections of drawings by Italian Renaissance artists, Ancient Egyptian artefacts, Chinese art, the coat belonging to Pocahontas' father, a ninth-century jewel made for King Alfred, and the lantern Guy Fawkes was using when he tried to blow up the Houses of Parliament. There is a rooftop restaurant and, in the basement, a café, shop and education centre (which often runs art workshops for children).

RANDOLPH HOTEL

In contrast to the Classical Ashmolean Museum opposite, the large five-star Randolph Hotel was built in the Victorian Gothic style by William Wilkinson in 1864. The hotel is named after not Randolph Churchill (father of Winston), but Francis Randolph, who gave money to start a gallery in the Ashmolean Museum. There are 151 bedrooms, a restaurant, a drawing room where you can have afternoon tea, and a bar which was used by the TV detective Inspector Morse. Some of the real-life guests have included Prime Ministers and world leaders, such as American presidents Bill Clinton and Jimmy Carter. A major fire on 17th April 2015 started in the ground floor kitchens. The flames were sucked up the air vents and burnt the floors above. Hundreds of people watched as the roads were closed down and 14 fire engines arrived to tackle the blaze.

WORCESTER COLLEGE

Worcester College was the first college of the 18th century, and the first new college since Pembroke ninety years earlier. It was started in 1714 by Sir Thomas Cookes on the site of Gloucester Hall, whose 14th-century cottages are still there. Most of the college was designed by Nicholas Hawksmoor and George Clarke. The buildings were started in 1720, but were not finished until 1791. In the meantime, both the architects died (in the same year, 1736). At the end of Beaumont Street, you can see the hall on the left and the chapel on the right, both jutting out into the street. In the middle is a small courtyard and entrance with a clock above. These buildings, however, are just a small part of the 26-acre grounds, the largest in Oxford, which include a lake. Past students include the writer of *Watership Down* Richard Adams, the media tycoon Rupert Murdoch and the film composer Rachel Portman.

MARTYRS' MEMORIAL

The Martyrs' Memorial (1843) is the first of many Oxford buildings in the Victorian Gothic style and the first of several by the architect George Gilbert Scott. It was put up as a reaction to the Oxford Movement, which wanted to bring the Church of England closer to the Catholic religion. The monument remembers the three Church of England bishops, Hugh Latimer, Nicholas Ridley and Thomas Cranmer, who were burnt alive in 1555-6 on the orders of the Catholic Queen Mary, eldest daughter of Henry VIII. Around the corner in Broad Street, you can see the cross in the road (pictured below) that marks the spot where they were actually burnt. Some students have told tourists that the Martyrs' Memorial is the spire of a sunken cathedral!

ST JOHN'S COLLEGE

The first college on this site was St Bernard's College, set up in 1437 as a place for monks to study. This was closed down along with many monasteries by Henry VIII, because he wanted to replace the Catholic religion with the new Church of England. After Henry died, however, his Catholic daughter Mary became queen. In 1555, the same year in which two Church of England bishops were burnt alive in Oxford on Mary's orders (see the Martyrs' Memorial, page 8), Sir Thomas White, a rich Catholic merchant, set up St John's College. It runs along most of St Giles' (including the Lamb and Flag pub) and its huge gardens go back as far as Parks Road. The front quad is partly what is left over from St Bernard's College; the rest took eighty years to build. In the past, you could not be arrested by the university police if you stood behind the low wall in front of the entrance to St John's College.

EAGLE AND CHILD

This building was a playhouse for soldiers during the English Civil War (1642–49). A year after the war finished, it became a pub known as The Eagle and Child, taking the picture on its pub sign from the crest of the Earl of Derby. From the 1930s to the 1950s, a group of writers called the 'Inklings' used to meet here, including J. R. R. Tolkien (author of the *Lord of the Rings*) and C. S. Lewis (author of the *Narnia* stories). The pub is affectionately known as 'The Bird and Baby'.

CORNMARKET

GEORGE STREET	NORTH	BROAD STREET
Natwest (bank)		Waterstones (books)
Pandora (jewellery)		Boswell (dept. store)
KFC (fast food)		Pylones (gifts)
Itsu (fast food)		St Michael's Church
Virgin (mobile phones)		SHIP STREET
ST MICHAEL'S STREET		Change (currency)
Austin Reed (clothes)		Pret à Manger (café on
Timpson (shoe repairs)		site of Former New Inn)
Snappy Snaps (photos)		Burger King
White Stuff (clothes)		W H Smith
EE (mobile phones)		Next (clothes)
3 store (mobile phones)		River Island (clothes)
L'Occitaine (beauty)		Fat Face (clothes)
Clarks (shoes)		Carphone Warehouse
Clarendon House (offices)		MARKET STREET
Gap (clothes)		Vodafone
CLARENDON CENTRE		Boots
H. Samuel (jewellery)		Starbucks
Barclays (bank)		Change (currency)
Champion Recruitment		West Cornwall Pasty Co.
EE (mobile phones)		GOLDEN CROWN (arcade)
McDonald's (fast food)		David Clulow (opticians)
Crown Pub		Reebok (sports)
Moss (clothes)		Pret à Manger (café)
HSBC (bank)		Lloyds (bank)
QUEEN STREET	SOUTH	HIGH STREET

ST MICHAEL'S CHURCH

Together with the Castle tower, St Michael's Church tower is one of the oldest buildings in Oxford, dating from Saxon times (1040). It was originally at the North Gate of the city, which was pulled down in 1771. Next to the tower on top of the North Gate, there was a prison called the Bocardo, where the bishops Latimer, Ridley and Cranmer were imprisoned in 1555 (see the Martyrs' Memorial on page 8). Inside the church you can see the pulpit used by John Wesley (who started the Methodist religion), the font where William Shakespeare stood as a godfather, and stained glass dating from the 13th century. You can also climb St Michael's tower for spectacular views across the city.

FORMER NEW INN

At 26-28 Cornmarket (on the corner of Ship Street) stands a three-floored timber-framed medieval building, with each of its two upper floors sticking out above the one below. This started life as the New Inn. James Gibbes, mayor of Oxford, began to build it in around 1386 and it was finished by his son ten years later. The inn was later known as the Blue Anchor; the diary of an Oxford man, Anthony Wood, says he saw a play here. In the 18th century, the innkeeper used to give everyone boarding the coach to Bath a glass of port for the journey. The medieval front of the building was changed in the 19th century. From the 1880s to the 1980s, this was the shop Joel Zacharias, Waterproof Manufacturers, known as 'Zacs for Macs' for short. It was then restored to its former glory, thanks to half a million pounds given by Jesus College, which owns the building.

BROAD STREET

CORNMARKET	MAGDALEN STREET
Waterstones (books)	
Boswell (department store)	
Wendy's News	
Fudge Kitchen	
Cath Kidston	
Watson's (souvenirs)	Balliol College
Oxford Campus Stores (souvenirs)	
The Buttery	
Isola (clothes)	
The Varsity Shop (souvenirs)	
Aidan Meller (art)	
Visitor Information Centre	
Oxfam	
Flaggs (souvenirs)	
Café	
Broad Canvas (arts)	
Inner Space (Yoga, Meditation)	Trinity College
Morton's (café)	
TURL STREET	
Blackwell's Art and Poster Shop	Blackwell's (books)
Exeter College	
Museum of History of Science	
Sheldonian Theatre	
Clarendon Building	Weston Library

14

BALLIOL COLLEGE

Balliol College was set up in about 1263 by Sir John de Balliol to say sorry for arguing with a bishop. It is the oldest college in Oxford to stay in the same place, although none of the original buildings are still there. The library is the oldest building, dating from 1431, but most of the Victorian Gothic buildings on Broad Street were designed by Alfred Waterhouse in 1868. Famous past students include three British Prime Ministers (Herbert Asquith, Harold Macmillan and Ted Heath); writers Hilaire Belloc, Graham Greene and Aldous Huxley; BBC presenters Robert Peston, Stephanie Flanders and Peter Snow; and politicians Roy Jenkins, Yvette Cooper and Boris Johnson.

TRINITY COLLEGE

Trinity College was started by Sir Thomas Pope in 1555 on the site of the medieval Durham College. The oldest part of Trinity College is called Durham Quad and the only building surviving from Durham College is the library (1421). The Durham Quad was followed by the Garden Quad (1668), the Front Quad (1887) and the Cumberbatch Quad (1968). Trinity College used to brew the best beer in Oxford to stop its students drinking in the city. According to legend, the back gates of Trinity College on Parks Road will only be opened when a Stuart (Catholic) monarch returns to the throne. This is unlikely to happen because the gates are actually railings which cannot be opened. Famous past students include two British Prime Ministers (Pitt the Elder and Lord North) and writers Miles Kington and Terence Rattigan.

BLACKWELL'S BOOKSHOP

When Benjamin Blackwell opened his bookshop in 1879, only three customers could fit in at the same time. Nowadays the bookshop spreads over four floors, including the Norrington Room under Trinity College, which has three miles of shelving space for sciences, business, economics and education. On the ground floor are fiction, local interest and children's books. On the first floor are literature, languages, poetry, biography and cookery books and a café overlooking Broad Street. On the second floor are history, classics and second-hand books. There is a music shop next door (on the other side of the White Horse pub) and an art and poster shop across the road.

SHELDONIAN THEATRE

The Sheldonian Theatre was built in 1668 by Christopher Wren (who later rebuilt many London churches, including St Paul's Cathedral, after the Great Fire of London). The building is designed in the Classical style and based on the Theatre of Marcellus in Rome. It is named after Gilbert Sheldon, the chancellor of the university at the time, who gave money for a building for university ceremonies, which still take place here, along with lectures and concerts (but not plays, despite its name). It is guarded by 17 Emperor's Heads on pillars. The 21m by 24m roof is held up by a clever structure of wooden beams, hidden above a painted ceiling showing a person representing 'Truth expelling Ignorance from the University'. You can walk up to the attic to admire Wren's timber beams and the lantern to admire the view over central Oxford.

WESTON LIBRARY

The New Bodleian Library (as it was first called) was designed by Sir Giles Gilbert Scott, the grandson of George, architect of the Martyrs' Memorial (Giles also designed the famous red British public telephone boxes). Its five floors above the ground and three below were built to store the ever-growing collection of books in the Bodleian Library, and is joined to the main library by an underground tunnel with a 'conveyor' for transporting books. The building was completed in 1940 and opened by King George VI in 1946, when the silver key broke in the door. You can see the broken key, along with Shakespeare's First Folio, the Magna Carta, and many other delights, in the treasury, part of a new public space which opened on 21 March 2015. The library was renamed because of a gift from the Garfield Weston Foundation.

CLARENDON BUILDING

Oxford University Press, the second-oldest university press in the world (after Cambridge), started in about 1480. In 1668, it moved to the attic of the newly-built Sheldonian Theatre. The Clarendon Building, the first of many Classical designs by Nicholas Hawksmoor in Oxford, was built in 1713 to house the printing press. From 1832, it was used as university offices and in 1975 became part of the ever-growing Bodleian Library. The Clarendon Building has a grand entrance and, on the roof, statues of the nine Muses (Ancient Greek goddesses who were believed to inspire art, music and literature). Oxford University Press moved to its current buildings on Walton Street in 1826, where today is the biggest university printing press in the world.

INDIAN INSTITUTE

The Indian Institute was built by Basil Champneys in 1883 for people to learn more about India, where Britain had an empire from 1858 to 1947. There are many Indian details on the building, like the weather vane in the shape of an elephant, a sign in the ancient Indian language of Sanskrit in the entrance, and Hindu gods and animals on the walls. In 1968, Oxford University took over the building to house the History department of the Bodleian Library. This upset the Indian government, because the building had been paid for by British and Indian people for studying India. Since 2013, the building houses the Oxford Martin School, which studies ways of making the whole world better in the future.

MUSEUM OF THE HISTORY OF SCIENCE

This is the oldest museum in the world to have remained a museum until the present day. It started in 1683 as the Ashmolean Museum. In 1924, the Museum collection was moved to Beaumont Street and the building on Broad Street became the Museum of the History of Science. It has a collection of early scientific instruments unlike any other, including astrolabes and telescopes for looking at the stars, machines for doing maths before calculators were invented, and old-fashioned chemistry sets. In the basement is the blackboard on which Albert Einstein wrote in 1931 when giving a lecture in Oxford to explain the expansion of the universe

EXETER COLLEGE

On the corner of Broad Street and Turl Street is Exeter College, the fourth oldest college in Oxford. It was started in 1314 by Walter Stapledon, Bishop of Exeter, although the oldest building existing today is Palmer's Tower (1432). The hall was built in 1618 and the front quad was completed in 1704. The Victorian Gothic chapel was designed by Sir George Gilbert Scott in 1860 and inspired by the Saint-Chapelle Church in Paris. Part of the college buildings are used by Blackwell's Art and Poster Shop, on top of which is a half-tonne iron statue by Anthony Gormley (2009). Famous past students include the artist William Morris, Charles Parry (the composer of 'Jerusalem'), Roger Bannister (the first person to run a mile in under four minutes) and the writers Philip Pullman and Martin Amis. J. R. R. Tolkien was a fellow at Exeter College and wrote *The Lord of the Rings* here.

HOLYWELL MUSIC ROOM

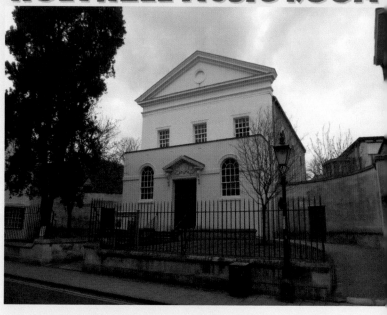

Built in 1748, the Holywell Music Room is Europe's first public concert hall. Within fifty years of being built, it had featured two famous composers: Handel and Haydn (who conducted his 'Oxford' Symphony here in 1791 before being given a special degree by the university). Although it was used as an auction house and library during the Victorian Era, it is once again used for musical performances today, including the Oxford Coffee Concerts on Sunday mornings, featuring world-class chamber music in a small venue at an affordable price (especially for children, who can go for free). The venue seats 250 people and is owned by Wadham College (see page 31).

TURF TAVERN

Hidden away from the streets by two narrow paths lies the Turf Tavern, a popular pub with indoor and outdoor seating. Its foundations date from the 13th century and its front bar from the 17th century. You can get to it from Bath Place (just off Holywell Street) or St Helen's Passage (just off New College Lane, near the Bridge of Sighs). St Helen's Passage used to be called Hell's Passage, where Jane Burden, wife and muse of William Morris, was born in 1838. The Turf Tavern has been visited by students who later became world leaders: former US president Bill Clinton and former Australian Prime Minister Bob Hawke, who set the world record for drinking a yard of ale (2½ pints) here in 11 seconds in 1953. In fiction, the Turf Tavern has been mentioned in *Brideshead Revisited* and the Inspector Morse books.

NEW COLLEGE

Started by William of Wykeham in 1379, this college was called 'new' so it could not be confused with Oriel College, as both were dedicated to the Virgin Mary. In 1394, Wykeham set up Winchester College, and its schoolboys (still called 'Wykehamists') were, for 460 years, the only boys who could go on to study at New College. The entrance is on New College Lane, although the college goes back as far as Longwall Street, Holywell Street and Queen's Lane, where you can see lots of gargoyles. The Warden from 1903-1924 was Dr Spooner, who was famous for mixing up the first letters of words. For example, he said to one of his students: 'You have hissed all my mystery lectures. You have tasted a whole worm. Please leave Oxford on the next town drain.'

MORRIS GARAGE

William Morris (1877-1963) started a bicycle repair business in his parents' shed in Oxford at the age of 16. He set up this garage in 1903, moving ten years later to the motor works at Cowley, the first in Britain to cheap cars on a large scale. William Morris received many honours, taking the name of Lord Nuffield after the Oxfordshire village where he lived. Lord Nuffield became very rich but he did not spend a lot of money on himself; instead, he gave 30 million pounds (about 700 million pounds in today's money) to good causes, including the Nuffield Foundation (to pay for hospitals) and Nuffield College (see page 62). His house near Henley-on-Thames, Nuffield Place, is kept as Lord Nuffield left it when he died in 1963. It is owned by the National Trust and open to the public.

HERTFORD COLLEGE

Elias de Hertford started Hart Hall in the 1280s. It became Hertford College in 1740, but by 1805 it stopped being a college because it ran out of money. In 1816 it became Magdalen Hall and in 1874 it become Hertford College again after the banker Thomas Baring gave money for it to be rebuilt. Thomas Jackson built most of what we see today, starting with the front part in 1887 and ending with the Bridge of Sighs in 1913. (It is called the Bridge of Sighs after a bridge of the same name in Venice, where condemned criminals would sigh on the way to prison. Perhaps modern day students also sigh on this bridge on their way to lectures.) Past students include the newsreader Fiona Bruce, Jonathan Swift, the writer of *Gulliver's Travels*, and Evelyn Waugh, whose novel *Brideshead Revisited* was partly filmed at Hertford College.

BODLEIAN LIBRARY

Thomas Bodley started the university library in 1602. In 1610, it was agreed that the library should receive a copy of every book published in Britain. The library is three floors high and shaped around a quadrangle. The Tower of Five Orders (1613–1624) has columns in five different styles of Greek and Roman architecture: from bottom to top: Tuscan, Doric, Ionic, Corinthian and Composite (a mixture of Ionic and Corinthian).. On the second-highest level is a statue of King James I. In front of the Divinity School (see next page) is a statue of William Herbert, the third Earl of Pembroke. He was Chancellor of Oxford University. The first published collection of Shakespeare's works, known as the First Folio, was dedicated to him (and possibly Shakespeare's sonnets as well). The head on the statue turns all the way around and can be taken off (although you're not allowed to try it!).

DIVINITY SCHOOL

Built in the Perpendicular Gothic style in 1488, this is the oldest university building (in other words, one that does not belong to any college) that still stands today. It was used for lectures about religion. There are nearly 100 coats of arms on the beautiful vaulted ceiling. The door on the north side was built by Christopher Wren in 1669 as a direct route to the Sheldonian Theatre. Above the Divinity School, and also built in 1488, is Duke Humfrey's Library, which became the oldest part of the Bodleian Library. The Divinity Schools have been used in two Harry Potter films (the hospital in *The Philosopher's Stone* and the dancing classroom in *The Goblet of Fire*. Duke Humfrey's Library was the library in *The Philosopher's Stone* and *The Chamber of Secrets*.

WADHAM COLLEGE

When Sir Nicholas Wadham, a Somerset gentleman, died in 1609, he left his fortune to the start a new college in Oxford. His 75-year-old widow, Dorothy, hired a builder and designed the college straight away – it was finished only four years later.

On the other side of the front quad from the entrance is a tower with statues of the king at the time, James I, and Nicholas and Dorothy Wadham underneath. Wadham also owns Holywell Music Room (see page 24). Former students include the TV and radio arts presenter Melvyn Bragg and the actress Rosamund Pike.

31

KEBLE COLLEGE

Opposite the Museum of Natural History on Parks Road are the multicoloured brick buildings of Keble College. The college started in 1870 for poor students training to become priests. It was named after John Keble, one of the leaders of the Oxford Movement, which wanted to bring the Church of England closer to the Catholic Church. The building was designed by William Butterfield and finished in 1882, the first new college to be built in Oxford since Worcester College almost 160 years earlier. The painter William Holman Hunt gave his picture *The Light of the World* to the chapel, but he was so angry when he found out the college was making people pay to see it that he painted a copy for St Paul's Cathedral in London. The students' rooms in Keble College are laid out along corridors instead of up and down staircases, like most Oxford colleges.

MUSEUM OF NATURAL HISTORY

The University Museum (as it was first called) was built in 1860 in the Victorian Gothic style, with a glass roof supported by iron columns. The art critic John Ruskin liked its design so much that he helped put up one of the columns. (He didn't do a very good job, as a workman pulled it down and put it back up again.) In the year the museum opened, there was a famous debate about the Theory of Evolution. The museum contains many birds and animals, including dinosaurs and a dodo.

33

PITT RIVERS MUSEUM

At the back of the Museum of Natural History is the Pitt Rivers Museum, a weird and wonderful collection of man-made objects from around the world. General Augustus Pitt Rivers gave his collection of 22,000 items to the university in 1884; this has since grown to half a million. Look out for the 12-metre-high totem pole made out of a single tree and the shrunken heads (pictured). The museum is said to have inspired Diagon Alley in the *Harry Potter* books.

RADCLIFFE CAMERA

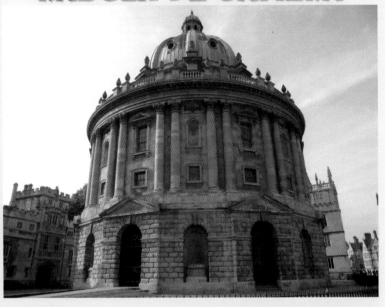

The round, domed 'Rad Cam' was named after John Radcliffe, who gave the money for it and built by James Gibbs in the Classical style in 1748. It was first called the Radcliffe Library for science books, but was later called the Radcliffe Camera when it became the main reading room of the Bodleian Library ('camera' is Latin for 'room'). The Radcliffe Camera is joined to the main part of the Bodleian Library by an underground tunnel called the Gladstone Link. There is a story of a drunken professor trying to find his way back to Brasenose College by feeling his way around the railings five times. In the Victorian comic novel *Verdant Green*, the student of the title is being shown around Oxford by a guide who wants to play a joke on him. 'This round building is the Vice-Chancellor's house,' he says. 'He has to go each night up to that balcony on the top, and look round to see if all's safe.'

BRASENOSE COLLEGE

Brasenose Hall, which started in the 13th century, was named after the brazen (or brass) nose, its door knocker in the shape of an animal's nose (pictured below). In 1333, a group of scholars unhappy with studying in Brasenose Hall went to Stamford, Lincolnshire and set up their own rival college there, taking the door knocker with them. Brasenose College started in 1509 on the same site as Brasenose Hall. When the college in Stamford came up for sale in 1890, they bought the whole building, just so they could get the door knocker back, over 550 years later. It now hangs proudly above above the high table in the hall (dining room). Most of the college buildings were designed by Thomas Jackson.

TURL STREET

BROAD STREET

Elmer Cotton Sports	Blackwell's Art and Poster
Turl Street Kitchen	Shop
Jesus College	Exeter College
MARKET STREET	**BRASENOSE LANE**
Norah's Antiques	
Oxfam books	
The Missing Bean (café)	
Turl Street News	
Rowell (jewellery)	Lincoln College
Walters (clothes)	
The Whisky Shop	
Ducker and Son (shoes)	
The Leather Shop	
Scripton (stationery)	
The Mitre Inn	All Saints' Church

HIGH STREET

37

LINCOLN COLLEGE

Between Brasenose Lane and the High Street is Lincoln College. It was started in 1427 by the Bishop of Lincoln to train priests to 'defend the mysteries of Scripture'. This was because the Bible had been translated into English for the first time by John Wycliffe (who had also been at Oxford). The Bishop died three years later, so money to build the college was slow to come in, but by 1475 the Front Quad was completed and is still there today, one of the best-preserved medieval colleges. The Chapel Quad was built in 1608-31 and the library in 1907. In 1975, the college took over All Saint's Church on the High Street as its new library. Past fellows include John Radcliffe, who gave money to build the Radcliffe Camera and the Radcliffe Infirmary and John Wesley, who started the Methodist religion. Past students include John le Carré, writer of spy books, Dr Seuss, writer of children's books, and the actress Emily Mortimer.

ALL SAINTS' CHURCH

On the corner of Turl Street and the High Street is All Saints' Church. The original church was built here in 1122, but fell down in 1700. A new building was designed by Henry Aldrich, Dean of Christ Church, in the Renaissance style. It was paid for by several people including Queen Anne and the first Duchess of Marlborough (living in the newly-built Blenheim Palace just outside Oxford) and completed in 1710. The tower and spire were added by Nicholas Hawksmoor ten years later. After St Martin's Church was demolished in 1896 (apart from its tower – see Carfax Tower on page 57), All Saints' became the City Church, a function taken over by St Michael's in 1971. All Saints' became the library of Lincoln College in 1975. The outside of the building was not changed at all, but the floor inside was raised by just over a metre to make room for a reading room in the basement.

JESUS COLLEGE

Jesus College is between Turl Street, Ship Street and Market Street, on the site of the medieval White Hall. It is the only college in Oxford to date from Elizabeth I's reign, and indeed was started by the Queen herself in 1571 because a Welshman, Hugh Price, asked her for a college in Oxford for Welsh students. (From the 1870s a wider range of students were admitted into the college, and nowadays about 15 in every 100 of its students are Welsh.) The college's three quads were built over the hundred years after it was started, although The Turl Street front was refaced in the Gothic Revival style by John Buckler in 1856. Famous past students include Lawrence of Arabia and Prime Minister Harold Wilson. Jesus College was the first men's college to accept women, in 1974 (the last was Oriel in 1985).

HIGH STREET (WEST)

CARFAX

Edinburgh Woollen Mill
Crew Clothing Co.
Paul (bakers)
Fellows (souvenirs)
Karen Millen (clothes)
Reiss (clothes)
Jigsaw (clothes)
Hays (recruitment)
Hotel Chocolat (shop)
Payne and Son (jewellers)
White Stuff (clothes)
At Thai (restaurant)
Northern Rock (bank)
Starbucks (café)
QL Delicatessen
Black Sheep Galleries
All Bar One (bar)
Phase Eight (clothes)

ALFRED STREET

Nat West (bank)
Coutts (bank)
Ede and Ravenscroft
 (academic dress)
Breckon and Breckon (estate agents)
OUP Bookshop
Hobbs (clothes)
Gerry Webber (clothes)
The Varsity Shop (souvenirs)
Shepherd+Woodward

KING EDWARD ST

Sweaty Betty
A-Plan Insurance
University of Oxford shop
Glasshouse
Sanders (prints and maps)
Toast (clothes)
Brora

Lloyds Bank
Jack Wills (clothes)
Reed (recruitment)
Whistles (clothes)
Rymans (stationery)

COVERED MARKET

L.K.Bennett (clothes)
Pizza Hut
Caffè Nero

COVERED MARKET

Whittards (tea/coffee)
Pia (jewellery)
Brook Street (recruitment)

COVERED MARKET

Tim's Newsagent
The Mitre Hotel

TURL STREET

All Saints' Church

Taylor's (delicatessen)
Oxford Blue (souvenirs)
Aspire (accessories)
Scrivens Opticians

Brasenose College

41

HIGH STREET (EAST)

ORIEL STREET

Oriel College

MAGPIE LANE

Old Bank Hotel/Quod
Patisserie Valerie
University College

LOGIC LANE

Pod (gifts)
Antiques on High
The Grand Café
Examination Schools

MERTON STREET

Marco's New York Italian
 (restaurant)
Eastgate Hotel
Oxford Spires Barbers
Hoyles (games and puzzles)
Pens Plus
Oxford Rendezvous
Stanford House

ROSE LANE

Botanic Garden

ST MARY'S PASSAGE

St Mary's Church

CATTE STREET

All Souls College
Oxford High St Souvenirs
Reginald Davis (jewellers)
The Oxford Gallery (art)
Havana House (tobacconist)
High Street Barbers
The Queen's College

QUEEN'S LANE

Queen's Lane Coffee Hse
Olives (delicatessen)
Simply Sewing
Oxford Travel Shop
Sahara (clothes)
Fitrite (shoes)
Honey's (newsagent)
Oxford Blue (souvenirs)
The Rose (café)
Hardy's Original Sweet Shop
Padarok (gifts)
Neal's Yard Remedies
Brother's (beauty)
Taylor's (delicatessen)
BR Money (exchange)
Unigifts (souvenirs)

LONGWALL STREET

Magdalen College

MAGDALEN BRIDGE

ST MARY'S CHURCH

You can climb the 127 steps of St Mary's Church tower, the oldest part of the Church (1280), for great views of central Oxford. The 55-metre Decorated Gothic spire was added in 1315-25. The chapel on the north side was built in about 1328 by Adam de Brome, who also started Oriel College opposite the Church. In the 1320s, the university meeting-place on the east side of the church (it is now the Vaults Café). The chancel was built in 1463 in the late Perpendicular Gothic style and the nave was finished in 1510. The Baroque entrance porch, with its twisted pillars, was built in 1637. In 1555, the trial of the Oxford Martyrs (see page 8) took place here; Elizabeth I visited it 11 years later. In the 1830s, Newman and Keble gave sermons here that began the Oxford Movement, hoping to bring the Church of England closer to its Catholic roots.

EXAMINATION SCHOOLS

This is where Oxford University students sit their gruelling exams in the Trinity (summer) Term. Tradition dictates that they wear 'sub fusc', a formal black-and-white suit, which can get very hot in the summer! Outside the dreaded exam season, the rooms are used for lectures. The building was completed in 1882 and was designed by Thomas Jackson. The writing above the entrance reads 'Dominus Illuminatio Mea', the Latin for 'the Lord is my light', which is the motto of Oxford University. You can also see a professor giving a student his degree.

TWO COFFEE HOUSES

Facing each other on opposite sides of the High Street are the Grand Café and the Queen's Lane Coffee House. They are two of the oldest coffee houses in Britain.

The Queen's Lane Coffee House was started in 1654 and is the oldest coffee house that has remained a coffee house since it started, not only in Britain, but in the whole of Europe. It is famous for its all-day cooked English breakfasts.

The Grand Café is on the site of the the Angel Inn, where the oldest coffee house in Britain was started in 1650, although different shops have been on this site since then.

When the Angel Inn stopped in 1866, a shopkeeper called Frank Cooper set up a grocery shop there. Soon he started selling his wife's marmalade in the shop, and it became very popular. They opened a jam factory near the railway station and before long their Oxford Marmalade was known all over the world. It even makes an appearance halfway down the rabbit-hole in *Alice's Adventures in Wonderland*.

MAGDALEN COLLEGE

Magdalen (pronounced 'Maudlin') College was started in 1458 by William of Wayneflete; most of the buildings you can see from the High Street were built over the following fifty years (look out for the gargoyles). There are large grounds with a deer park and walks along the River Cherwell (pronounced 'Charwell'). Magdalen College has the tallest tower in Oxford (44m). At 6am on 1st May every year the chapel choir sings a Latin hymn and Tudor madrigals to the crowds below, many of whom have stayed up all night having a party. You can hire a punt from nearby Magdalen Bridge – make sure you stand at the shallow decked end, not the raised flat end (that's only in Cambridge). Past students of Magdalen College include Cardinal Wolsey (who went on to begin Christ Church) and the writers Oscar Wilde and John Betjeman (who was taught by C. S. Lewis, a fellow at the college).

BOTANIC GARDEN

This, the oldest Botanic Garden in the world, was started in 1621 on the site of a Jewish cemetery. At first, it was called the Physic Garden because it only grew plants for medicines. The three Baroque entrances were built in 1632–33 by Nicholas Stone, who also built the entrance porch of St Mary's Church four years later. Nowadays the Botanic Garden has 8000 types of plant, spread over the walled garden, the lower garden and the greenhouses. There is a yew tree that was planted in 1645, during the English Civil War. The Botanic Garden appears in several famous Oxford books, including Lewis Carroll's *Alice in Wonderland* (pictured as the background to the Queen's croquet ground), Evelyn Waugh's *Brideshead Revisited* (where Sebastian takes Charles for a walk after their first lunch together) and Philip Pullman's *The Amber Spyglass* (where Will and Lyra sit on a bench in parallel worlds).

UNIVERSITY COLLEGE

There was a legend that King Alfred began University College in 874, but it was really started in 1249 by William, Archdeacon of Durham. Even so, it is still the oldest college to start in Oxford. None of the original medieval buildings are still there; the Front Quad which can be seen from the High Street dates from 1634. The poet Percy Bysshe Shelley started studying at University College in 1810, but was told to leave a year later for publishing a pamphlet which said people did not have to believe in God. This was considered shocking at a time when all students were expected to go to church. University College later became proud of the poet and was given a full-size memorial statue in 1893, which can still be seen in the college. Other past students include the Oxford-born physicist Stephen Hawking, writer C. S. Lewis and the statesmen Bill Clinton and Bob Hawke (see Turf Tavern on page 25).

ALL SOULS COLLEGE

All Souls College was started in 1438 by Archbishop Henry Chichele and Henry VI to remember the men who had died in Henry V's wars against France. The front quad (which opens onto the High Street) and chapel were completed in 1443 and are the oldest parts of the college. The larger North Quad, with its twin towers, Hall and Codrington Library, was designed by Nicholas Hawksmoor in 1715 in the Gothic style, in order to blend in with the existing college buildings. Only people who already have a 'first' (highest degree class) from Oxford can apply to be members of All Souls College. They have to write four essays in three hours each. Every hundred years, the members of the college process around the college with blazing torches searching for a duck whilst singing a medieval song. This will happen next on 14 January 2101, so put the date in your diary.

THE QUEEN'S COLLEGE

The Queen's College was started in 1341 by Robert de Eglesfield, chaplain to Queen Philippa, the wife of Edward III, and was named after her. None of the original medieval buildings are still there. Christopher Wren designed the front quad in 1672 and the library in 1696; the rest of the college (including the High Street front) was designed by Nicholas Hawksmoor in the Classical style and built 1710-1756. The statue above the entrance is of Queen Caroline, the wife of George II, who gave money towards the new buildings. According to legend, a student at the medieval Queen's College saved himself from a wild boar by shoving a Greek book down its throat. Ever since then, the Queen's College has celebrated Christmas by bringing in a Boar's Head whilst singing the 'Boar's Head Carol'. Past students include King Henry V, comedian Rowan Atkinson (Mr Bean) and internet inventor Tim Berners-Lee.

ORIEL COLLEGE

Oriel, the fifth oldest college in Oxford, was started in 1326 by Adam de Brome as 'House of the Blessed Mary the Virgin in Oxford'. The college is called 'Oriel' after a house that used to be on the site and a type of window that sticks out from the wall – this can be seen above the entrance to the oldest part of the college, the front quad (1620–40). In the 1830s and 40s, two fellows of Oriel, John Keble and John Henry Newman, were part of the Oxford movement, which encouraged the Church of England to move closer to Roman Catholicism. Oriel was the last all-male college in Oxford: it started having female students from 1985. (The last all-female college was St Hilda's, which took men from 2008.) Past students include two explorers: Sir Walter Raleigh from the Elizabethan era and Cecil Rhodes from the Victorian era.

MERTON COLLEGE

Dating from 1264, Merton College was, ten years later, the first Oxford college to be recognised in law. It also has the oldest existing college buildings in Oxford. The ground floor of the chapel was built in 1290 (its bell tower was added in 1452). The library, built in 1373, is the oldest in Britain and the oldest university library in the world. Some of the oldest books are so precious that they have always been chained to the shelves. When the Fellows' Quad was built in 1610, the older quadrangle (1304-1378) housing the students became known as the 'Mob Quad' from the Latin 'mobile vulgus' ('fickle crowd'). From the cobbled Merton Street, there are several short cuts leading to the High Street and one leading to Merton Grove and Christ Church Meadow.

CORPUS CHRISTI COLLEGE

Between Merton College and Christ Church's Canterbury Gate lies Corpus Christi, Oxford's smallest college for undergraduates (students working towards their first degree). The college was started in 1517 by Bishop Richard Foxe, chief advisor to King Henry VIII. The front quad, which dates from that time, has a column with a sundial and the statue of a pelican on top, which is the symbol of the college. Corpus Christi was the first Oxford college to teach Ancient Greek — in fact, for many years all students had to learn the language. Every summer, Corpus Christi holds a Tortoise Race for charity. Past pupils include the the religious reformer John Keble and one-time Labour party leader Ed Milliband.

ST EDMUND HALL

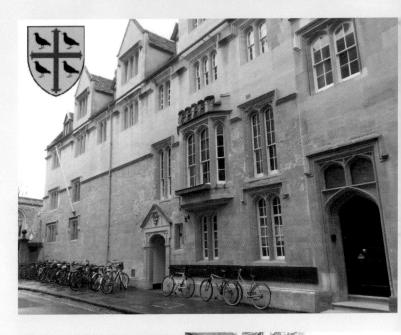

Dating from 1270, 'Teddy Hall' is one of the oldest places for studying in Oxford, but it did not become a college until 1957. The Norman church of St Peter-in-the-East, a little further down Queen's Lane, is now the  college library. Past students include Terry Jones of the Monty Python comedy group.

QUEEN STREET

WEST

WESTGATE CENTRE	BONN SQUARE
	NEW INN HALL STREET
Size	Beaverbrooks
Apricot	Accessorize
New Look	Jeans West
Goldsmiths	Costa (café)
ST EBBE'S STREET	East (clothes)
	Specsavers (opticians)
	Monsoon (clothes)
Holter	Paperchase
	Maxwell's (restaurant)
Marks and Spencer	Ryman (stationery)
	French Connection (clothes)
Topman/Topshop	**CLARENDON CENTRE**
	Cornish Kitchen
Flight Centre	Swarovski
	Nationwide
The White Company	Crabtree and Evelyn
Jones (shoes)	Carfax Tower
Eat (fast food)	
Santander (bank)	
ST ALDATE'S	**CORNMARKET**

EAST

CARFAX TOWER

Carfax (which comes from the Latin for 'crossroads') is where the High Street, Cornmarket, Queen Street and St Aldate's meet at the centre of Oxford. The 14th-century tower is all that remains of St Martin's Church, originally built in 1122. The rest of the church became unsafe so was rebuilt in the Gothic style in 1820, only to be knocked down in 1896, to make way for bigger crossroads at Carfax. William Shakespeare is said to have become godfather to William Davenant here (the font later went to All Saints' and then St Michael's Church). The two 'quarter boys' under the clock chime every quarter of an hour. You can climb the 99 steps for stunning views over Oxford from the top of the 23-metre high tower.

TOWN HALL

This, the third Town Hall on this site, built in 1897, was a modern building by Victorian standards, as it had central heating and electricity. It was designed by Thomas Hare and opened by the Prince of Wales (the future Edward VII). Some students fought in the streets about the arrangements for the opening and found themselves amongst the first prisoners in the new Town Hall cells. The building also includes the Main Hall (where the Rolling Stones played in 1964), the Assembly Rooms (used as restaurant during World War II, it is now used for wedding receptions), and the Council Chamber (with the signs of the zodiac on the ceiling). The Museum of Oxford on the south-west corner of the building used to be the library, before it moved to the Westgate Centre at the end of Queen Street.

CHRIST CHURCH

In 1525, Cardinal Wolsey set up Cardinal College. However, in 1529, King Henry VIII decided he didn't like Cardinal Wolsey any longer because he couldn't get the king a divorce from his first wife (Wolsey died a year later). In 1532, it was renamed King Henry VIII College and finally, in 1548, Christ Church, as part of the new Church of England (which *did* get the king a divorce). The college shares the site with Oxford's Cathedral, on the site of the chapel (1120) dedicated to St Frideswide, the patron saint of Oxford. Christopher Wren built Tom Tower in 1681-82. Its biggest bell, Great Tom, rings 101 times every night. This was because in the old days there were 101 students and they all had to be in college by 9 o'clock 'Oxford time' (which is actually 9.05pm for most people!). Charles I made Oxford the capital during the Civil War and lived in Christ Church (his queen lived in Merton College). The many famous past students include John and Charles Wesley (founders of the Methodist Church), Robert Hooke and Albert Einstein (scientists), Edward VII and 13 British Prime Ministers.

ALICE'S SHOP

Opposite Christ Church is a shop with a red front door where a girl called Alice Liddell used to buy her sweets in the 1860s. She was the daughter of the Dean of Christ Church, and she became friends with a maths fellow in the college called Charles Dodgson. On 4 July 1862, Charles took Alice and her two sisters on a boat trip down the Thames and told them a story about a girl called Alice who falls down a rabbit-hole and has lots of adventures. Three years later, using the pen-name Lewis Carroll, Charles published *Alice's Adventures in Wonderland*, which has since become one of the most popular children's books ever. Alice's Shop even appears in the follow-up book *Through the Looking-Glass* as the Old Sheep Shop, 'full of all manner of curious things'. Today you can buy souvenirs of Wonderland there.

PEMBROKE COLLEGE

Opposite Christ Church is the smaller Pembroke College, started in 1624 by Thomas Tesdale and Richard Wightwick as a college for boys from Abingdon School. The college was named after the Earl of Pembroke, who was Chancellor of the University at the time and whose statue is in the Old Schools Quad of the Bodleian Library (see page 29). The front on St Aldate's was first built by Cardinal Wolsey in 1525. The Old or Front Quad dates from 1670-99, the Baroque Chapel 1732, and the Chapel Quad from 1830. Pembroke's most famous student was Samuel Johnson (at the college 1728-29), who put together the first famous English dictionary. When he was fined as a student for missing a lecture, Johnson replied, 'Sir, you have fined me tuppence for missing a lecture that was not worth a penny'. He spent most of his time staying in his rooms drinking tea – Pembroke College still has his teapot.

OXFORD CASTLE

St George's Tower and St Michael's Tower in Cornmarket are the oldest buildings in Oxford and the only two Saxon defensive towers left in Britain. Although often described as Norman, the Saxons starting building St George's Tower in 1009, after the Vikings burnt Oxford to the ground. The rest of Oxford Castle was built in the Norman style in 1071 by Robert D'Oilly, a close friend of William the Conqueror, but only the mound remains. The castle has played an important part in two civil wars. The first of these, called the Anarchy (1135-1152) was between Stephen and Matilda, who was trapped in the tower for three months in 1142. Matilda escaped across the frozen River Thames, disguised by wearing a white robe in the snow. During the English Civil War (1642-1651) the castle was strengthened. It was used as a prison until 1996 and then converted into a tourist attraction and Malmaison Hotel.

NUFFIELD COLLEGE

In 1937, Lord Nuffield (see the Morris Garage, page 27) gave a million pounds for a new college for postgraduates (students who already had a degree) at the basin of the Oxford Canal. Because of the Second World War and building restrictions, Nuffield College was not started until 1949 and not finished until 1960. The 46-metre high square stone tower, housing the college library, is topped by a modern copper-covered version of Oxford's medieval 'dreaming spires'. The lower quad has a long rectangular pond overlooked by students' rooms. At first, Lord Nuffield wanted his college to be for engineering and accountancy (two very important areas of his own life) but he was persuaded to change this to social sciences. Although he complained about the delays in building the college, Lord Nuffield left the college the rest of his money and his home, Nuffield House, when he died in 1963.

HOW TO GET THERE

By car – Leave the M40 at junction 8 (if coming from London) or 9 (if coming from Birmingham). It is difficult and expensive to park in Oxford, so try the park-and-ride sites: Pear Tree and Water Eaton (north), Thornhill (east), Redbridge (south) or Seacourt (west). There are car parks on Worcester Street and Gloucester Green and short-term street parking available on St Giles' and Broad Street (accessible by car from Parks Road).

By air – Heathrow and Birmingham are the nearest airports. The Oxford Bus Company and National Express run frequent coach services from Gatwick and Heathrow to Oxford. You can get from Stanstead and Luton to Oxford on the 737 National Express coach.

By coach – the Oxford Bus Company (X90) and the Oxford Tube both run frequent coach services from London to Oxford, generally cheaper than the train. There are several pick-up/drop-off points in Oxford, including Gloucester Green coach station, the High Street, St Clement's and Headington.

By train – There are frequent direct rail services from London and Birmingham. Oxford railway station is 10 minutes' walk west of the city centre.

By bike – cycling is the quickest way to get around in Oxford – you can go where cars cannot, like the High Street, and there are many places to lock up your bike.

TOP 10 MUSEUMS

All free to enter unless it says otherwise.

1. Ashmolean Museum
2. Museum of Natural History
3. Pitt Rivers Museum
4. Weston Library
5. Oxford Castle (entrance charge)
6. Museum of the History of Science
7. Modern Art Oxford
8. Story Museum (entrance charge)
9. Museum of Oxford
10. Bate Collection of Musical Instruments

TOP 10 SHORT CUTS

Ten useful shortcuts where cars cannot go and the places that they join together.

1. New College Lane (Catte St/Queen's Lane)
2. Queen's Lane (High Street/New College Lane)
3. Magpie Lane (High Street/Merton Street)
4. Logic Lane (High Street/Merton Street)
5. Lamb and Flag Passage (St Giles'/Parks Road)
6. St Helen's Passage (New College Lane/Turf Tavern)
7. Grove Walk (Merton Street/Deadman's Walk)
8. Deadman's Walk (Merton College/Christ Church)
9. Bath Place (Holywell Street/Turf Tavern)
10. Brasenose Lane (Radcliffe Square/Turl Street)

DREAMING SPIRES

This is the view from Boar's Hill which inspired the poet Matthew Arnold to describe Oxford's 'dreaming spires'. Here are twelve of Oxford's tallest buildings:

1. St Mary's Church Spire 55m
2. Christ Church Cathedral Spire 46m
3. Nuffield College Spire 46m
4. Magdalen Tower 44m
5. Radcliffe Camera 43m
6. Christ Church, Tom Tower 41m
7. All Saints' Church 40m
8. All Souls College Twin Towers 39m
9. Exeter College Chapel Spire 37m
10. Oxford Castle, St George's Tower 30m
11. Carfax Tower 23m
12. Sheldonian Theatre 21m

OXFORD'S RECORDS

- First mile run in less than four minutes – Roger Bannister, 6 May 1953, Iffley Road Running Track
- First Oxfam shop (in Broad Street, 1949)
- Europe's first public concert hall – Holywell Music Room (1748)
- First Englishman to go up in a hot air balloon (James Sadler, 4 October 1784, Merton Grove)
- First identification of a human cell – Robert Hooke
- Invention of Boyle's Law
- Most British Prime Ministers at one university (26, 13 of whom went to Christ Church)
- Oldest coffee houses in Britain (see **Two Coffee Houses**)
- First cars mass-produced in Britain (Nuffield Motors)
- World's longest running scientific experiment (Electric Bell, Clarendon Laboratory, 1840 to present)
- Most Scrabble games played at once (28, Chris May, Oxford University Press, 2013)
- Only two Saxon defensive towers left in the Uk – St George's Tower (1009) and St Michael's Church (1040)

MYSTERY TOUR

By answering these questions, you can go on a pleasant one-hour walk beginning and ending on the High Street (with the option to visit the Turl Tavern halfway round). All the answers are somewhere in this book.

1. Which lane going off the High Street, is named after a bird?........................ Lane

2. Which street has cobbles? .... Street

3. What is the Latin motto of Oxford University, which appears above the entrance to the Exam Schools? (It means 'God is my light'.) ....

4. What is the name of the faces carved on the sides of old buildings to scare away evil spirits? ....

5. What is the name of the bridge that goes across New College Lane and links the two sides of Hertford College? ....

6. Whose statue is in the courtyard of the Bodleian Library? ....

7. What animal is on top of the Indian Institute?...............................

8. What is the name of the bookshop opposite the Sheldonian Theatre? ....

9. In which year was the Radcliffe Camera built?......................

10. How tall is the spire of St Mary's Church?...................metres

OXFORD COLLEGES

1. University 1249
2. Balliol 1263
3. Merton 1264
4. Exeter 1314
5. Oriel 1326
6. The Queen's 1341
7. New 1379
8. Lincoln 1427
9. All Souls 1438
10. Magdalen 1458
11. Brasenose 1509
12. Corpus Christi 1517
13. Christ Church 1546
14. St John's 1555
15. Trinity 1555
16. Jesus 1571
17. Wadham 1610
18. Pembroke 1624
19. Worcester 1714
20. Hertford 1740
21. Keble 1870
22. Lady Margaret Hall 1878
23. Somerville 1879
24. St Hugh's 1886
25. St Hilda's 1893
26. Nuffield 1937
27. St Anne's 1952
28. St Edmund Hall 1957
29. St Peter's 1961
30. Linacre 1962
31. St Antony's 1963
32. St Catherine's 1963
33. St Cross 1965
34. Wolfson 1981
35. Kellogg 1994
36. Mansfield 1995
37. Harris Manchester 1996
38. Green Templeton 2008

Permanent Private Halls

1. Wycliffe Hall 1877
2. Campion Hall 1896
3. St Benet's Hall 1897
4. Blackfriars 1921
5. Regent's Park College 1927
6. St Stephen's House 2003

WORDSEARCH

Can you find all 38 Oxford Colleges in this wordsearch?

```
H  M  S  T  C  R  O  S  S  L  T  C  N  L  Z  S  U  K  E  N
C  A  E  L  L  I  V  R  E  M  O  S  I  E  N  E  L  E  K  L
R  N  R  F  S  L  Y  I  K  K  H  N  N  H  B  L  N  B  O  O
U  S  O  R  C  T  R  T  E  E  A  S  O  T  A  E  O  L  R  C
H  F  Q  S  I  O  H  S  I  C  L  J  A  H  O  T  T  E  B  N
C  I  U  C  F  S  N  I  R  S  T  L  T  N  Y  D  E  S  M  I
T  E  E  O  O  L  M  E  L  S  R  E  O  P  O  X  L  E  E  L
S  L  E  O  E  R  O  A  S  D  R  E  R  G  E  T  P  N  P  S
I  D  N  Y  B  M  P  W  N  A  A  R  V  T  G  O  M  I  E  L
R  T  S  I  A  A  S  U  G  C  W  S  E  I  U  D  E  R  S  U
H  T  R  H  T  U  L  R  S  O  H  R  O  E  N  A  T  E  O  O
C  I  D  I  S  G  A  L  R  C  S  E  D  A  F  U  N  H  N  S
P  A  N  E  N  M  D  C  I  N  H  H  S  R  T  N  E  T  E  L
W  S  J  S  Y  I  E  R  N  O  O  R  G  T  I  W  E  A  S  L
I  E  A  D  R  S  T  C  O  E  L  T  I  U  E  O  R  C  A  A
S  T  A  N  T  O  N  Y  S  F  W  U  R  S  H  R  G  T  R  O
B  L  S  E  S  R  E  T  E  P  T  S  H  E  T  T  N  S  B  M
S  S  R  N  U  F  F  I  E  L  D  R  N  H  M  I  S  E  H  T
S  T  E  D  M  U  N  D  H  A  L  L  E  S  T  A  N  N  E  S
N  E  L  A  D  G  A  M  I  O  I  T  H  H  A  M  R  N  C  G
```

STREET MAP

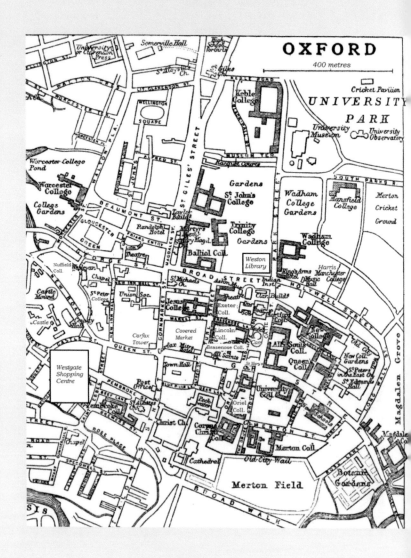

Printed in Great Britain
by Amazon